Tall Ships

Tall Ships

Text by Kathryn Lasky

Photographs by Christopher G. Knight

Charles Scribner's Sons   New York

Acknowledgment for the use of photographs is made to the Peabody Museum of Salem (pages 11, 19, 22, 29, 35, 36, 45, and 49), to the Penobscot Marine Museum of Searsport, Maine (pages 25 and 48), to Martin Sandler of the Sandler Collection (page 17), to John E. Thayer (pages 6 and 58), and to David W. Harp (pages 30, 31, 39, 46, and 61).

Library of Congress Cataloging in Publication Data
Lasky, Kathryn.
Tall ships.
SUMMARY: Discusses the tall ships which sailed the world before the advent of steam. Describes how they were built, the men who built and sailed them, and life aboard.
1. Sailing Ships. 2. Navigation. 3. Seafaring life. [1. Sailing ships. 2. Seafaring life] I. Knight, Christopher G. II. Title.
VK149.L37 387.2′2 78-14580
ISBN 0-684-15964-3

1 3 5 7 9 11 13 17 19 MD/C 20 18 16 14 12 10 8 6 4 2

Printed in the United States of America

We wish to thank William Pendleton, grandson of Captain Andrew Pendleton, and his wife Mary, for helping us come to know this remarkable man.

For

PETE KNIGHT

who gave us a love of the sea

Boston Harbor July 10, 1976

One

The wind had been blowing out of the west, a land breeze, all that morning in Boston. But shortly before ten o'clock it changed to east, a wind from the sea, and with it came the tall ships, their canvas sails billowing softly in the breeze. They glided into the old port as they had so many times before, but the year was not 1776 or 1876. It was July 10, 1976, and 600,000 people who had never seen a tall ship lined the waterfront of Boston awaiting their return.

Tall ships had been sailing before there were buttons to push and switches to turn for power, when people had to fit their lives to nature. They had only the wind and the skill of men who knew the ways of the sea. The sailing trade had become part of everyday life, and adventurous people from merchants to cabin boys made it possible. Livelihoods depended on the tall ships that followed the wind routes of the water world to China, Australia, and India to bring home the goods Americans wanted.

In the colonial days Americans had relied on English ships to bring from China the teas, silks, and nankeen cloth which they enjoyed so much. In exchange they shipped out lumber and codfish and shoes. After the Revolutionary War, adventurous New England merchants wasted little time acquiring their own ships and exploring new trading markets all over the world. They had a shrewd eye for anything that could bring a higher price in another part of the world, and they had the ships to move goods to the market. Cod and lumber and candles were no longer their only trading goods. They would travel now to Madeira and the Azores to pick up a cargo of wine or to Mediterranean ports for fruit, then to a South American port where these products were exchanged for mahogany that could be traded in Calcutta for cotton or in Sumatra for pepper, which in turn could then be traded in Canton for teas, silks, and porcelains. The goal was to make a profit on each cargo and thus to increase the total profit of the enterprise. "Increase" was the name of the trading game, and to increase one's investment was considered such a virtuous occupation that many baby boys born at this time were given the word as a name. It was as if parents hoped that merely by naming the child Increase they could turn him in the direction of commercial success in life.

So these ships went clipping around the world, crossing every sea, swapping all sorts of stuff in all kinds of ports. The captains or supercargoes (clerks of the cargo) had the authority to do the trading in ports, on the basis of written instructions from the ship's owner at the beginning of a voyage. An owner's letter might direct the captain in the following way:

Captain Joseph, Master of The Ship *Endurance*

As soon as possible:

Leave for Madagascar with a stop at the Cape of Good Hope, if you make a fast passage. If your passage is slow don't stop. If you do stop and can sell your cargo at a ten percent profit, buy 2,000 cattle hides and any other goods which will sell at a 40% higher price at home. If you can do this, proceed directly home with a stop at St. Helena for any additional hides.

If you can sell the ship at the Cape of Good Hope for more than $4,000, do this and take payment in hides which you should send home in any other ship bound to Massachusetts.

If you get to Madagascar, sell your cargo at the best possible price, and if you can sell the ship for $3,000 and buy other goods and ship them home on another vessel do this. We hope you'll get $5,000 or $6,000 for the ship.

If you can buy cotton cloth, take it to Belgium and send it on to London on British ships. Bring freight home.

8

Keep clear records of your transactions. If anything happens to you we appoint Jonathan Rice, the mate, to take command. We hope you will have a successful voyage, with God's protection.

William Nicholson

P.S. Don't take French currency as payment. It is too risky.

A ship's captain could swap just about anything, including the ship itself, as long as a profit was made. The officers of a ship were allowed cargo space for up to five tons for their own private "adventures." Captain Jacob Crowninshield filled his allowance almost completely on one trip when he imported the first elephant to this country from India and sold it for ten thousand dollars, making a fantastic profit.

Of all the trading ports in the world, Canton was a very special one. It was located up the Canton River, eighty miles from the coast. No "white she-devils," as the Chinese called the English and American women, were allowed into the city, so wives and daughters of traders were forced to stay in Macao, a Portuguese settlement near the coast, while the men went to Canton for the six-month trading season. One young woman who accompanied her brother and his wife on a voyage to China, however, refused to stay in Macao without even glimpsing the Celestial City of Canton. To have come all the way from Salem, Massachusetts, and not to see China was unthinkable to Harriet Low. She and her sister-in-law, disguised as boys in caps and cloaks, boarded a riverboat and went up to Canton. In her diary Harriet wrote: "Here we are in the Celestial City, but the Hong merchants are making a row and it is doubtful whether we remain for long." The Chinese officials had issued a "chop," or statement, she said, warning that all trade in Canton would stop "if one Low did not immediately remove his family to Macao."

Harriet and her sister-in-law were not easily frightened off and did manage to stay for several days. They saw a great deal of Canton, and Harriet wrote lively descriptions of the amazing city. She saw huge tea boats lined up in Canton Harbor so as to form complete "streets" on the water, a floating city of boats all lacquered in bright paint and decorated with colorful silk pennants. She describes the harbor at night in the soft light of a million paper lanterns strung across the decks of tea and flower boats.

From the very beginning of the China trade there was one big problem. The Chinese had no need to trade at all, for their land was so rich and fertile that they could produce almost everything they wanted. The foreign traders from Britain and America had to be able to offer something that the Chinese would want and need, a cargo to exchange for the silks and teas and porcelains that were so popular and profitable at home.

In the earliest days of the China trade, American ships would arrive in Canton with cases of ginseng, a plant that the Chinese believed was good for their health. But soon the market was glutted with ginseng and the price dropped. American traders next turned to sealskins, then to otter fur, both of which were popular with the Chinese for a time; but as with all fashions, these went out of style in a few years—after all, they had never been truly needed. There was one cargo, however, that both British and Americans could count on to get the highest price, and the market instead of becoming glutted, demanded more and more as use of the product grew uncontrollably. The precious cargo was opium, an illegal drug that ruined millions of lives in China. Merchants who would sell anything for a profit found opium to be pure gold. Chinese addicts created an insatiable market for it, a market supplied by a well-organized network of Chinese smugglers who met foreign ships outside of Canton and took delivery of the opium.

By 1830 there were millions of opium smokers in China, and it seemed impossible to break the trade. Although the United States imported less opium into China than did the British, every American trading company that could get opium traded it in Canton, with the exception of one—the Olyphant Company—which steadfastly refused to have anything to do with the opium trade. Other American companies made substantial profits from the sale of opium, most of which they bought in Turkey. Few people questioned the morality of dealing in this harmful drug. Missionaries

Opium ships in the harbor of Lintin, China, in 1824. The multi-oared boat on the extreme right is the type the Chinese opium smugglers used for rowing ashore quickly with their cargo

sailing to China from America to save the souls of the "poor heathen Chinese" probably gave little thought to the deadly cargo of the ships on which they were traveling. It was a fact of life, then as now, that profit was the goal of the trade: just as well a chest of opium as an elephant in the cargo hold.

A form of trade carried on at an even more terrible cost of human life was the importation of slaves. Although there were strict laws in New England against the importation of slaves, some vessels did slip on board what traders callously called "Black Ivory" when they docked in West Africa to buy palm oil. In the South the slave trade was not illegal, so hundreds of American and British ships would enter South Carolina, Georgia, and Louisiana each year loaded with their tragic cargo of human beings for sale.

Not all trading, however, was carried on with such disregard for human life, and many a profit was made in an honest way that

11

benefited people. One of the most ingenious merchants dealt in a thoroughly decent product that could only help people, yet everyone laughed and said "Impossible!" when Frederick Tudor first tried to ship a hundred tons of ice to the hot West Indies. He was called crazy and worse; but he had heard of the plague of yellow fever that had swept away whole towns in the West Indies in 1805 and nearly wiped out the crews of the European fleets stationed there. He knew that ice, if it had been available, would have relieved some suffering. That winter he cut tons of ice from his pond outside of Boston, and loaded these "crystal blocks of Yankee coldness," as someone called them, onto his brig, *Favorite*, to sail for the island of Martinique. A crew was hard to find; most sailors were convinced that the ice would melt and swamp the ship. Despite taunts and predictions of failure, Frederick Tudor succeeded in delivering his cargo in perfect condition. It was the start of a successful business. Tudor packed the ice in sawdust for insulation, and he even imbedded apples in the great chunks, so that the fruits arrived fresh and crisp to ports that had never tasted them.

Tudor became known as the Ice King and gradually managed to push his business into the East Indies and Calcutta. It took courage to send tons of ice on a four- or five-month voyage that crossed the fiery equator, doubled the Horn, and passed through that furnace of a sea, the Indian Ocean. In his diary Frederick Tudor wrote of his daring adventure:

> I began this trade in the youthful hopes attendant on the age of twenty-two. I have followed it until I have a head with scarcely a hair that is not white. . . . I found myself without money and without friends, and with only a cargo of ice in a torrid zone to depend on for the supply of both. . . .

Later he wrote with humor about his strange enterprise:

> Thus is the winter of my discontent made glorious summer. . . . Drink, Spaniard, and be cool, that I who have suffered so much in the cause may be able to go home and keep myself warm.

Whether the cargo was ice, opium, tea, slaves, silk, or elephants, the most important thing for a merchant was to be the first, or as near as possible to the first, on the market with his product. To accomplish this, fast ships were needed, for the cargo that was first to the unloading dock drew the highest price. As the competition increased for cargo trade, so did the speed of the ship. The tea clippers were built with emphasis on speed rather than on the size of the cargo they could carry. Speed was needed—speed for Hong Kong or speed for California and the Gold Rush.

Two

As hull shapes became sharper to increase a tall ship's speed through the water, more sails were added to harness more power from the wind. And for more sails, a ship needed more masts. There was hardly room for more masts on the deck, so designers began to set them atop one another.

When masts sprouted skyward like trees, designers had to invent more and more names for the new sails. Naming was easy enough at the lower part of the masts. There was a pattern: A sail was named after the mast that carried it. So a foresail flew from the foremast and a mainsail from the mainmast. When the designers set a mast on top of one of these lower masts, they very sensibly called it a topmast and the sail a topsail. But they built a mast even higher than the topmast, so they had to think up a name that sounded even higher and loftier—really tall, but not the tallest (because they still had plans). They finally decided to call this mast the topgallant and the sails topgallant sails.

Designers kept on building and added one mast that was the highest of all, one that reached nearly two hundred feet into the sky. This they called the royal mast, and the sail was called a top royal. But the clipper ships, those "China birds" that flashed across the seas to Canton and Shanghai, dared to fly sails even above the royals, and these were called skysails and moonrakers, for how much higher could you go?

The first step in shipbuilding began in the New England forest. A young woodsman—ten years old, perhaps, only a boy—walked

14

Left: *The forward three masts of the Russian bark* Kruzenstern, *all with square yards. The crew is in the rigging readying to unfurl the sails.*
Right: *The* Kruzenstern *unfurls her foresail*

quickly through the forest searching with his expert eyes for the right larch or hackmatack trees. When he spotted one, he would know at once that what grew before him was not just a tree but the foundation for a full-rigged ship. The right hackmatacks would have the natural bend of "ribs" and "knees" that were the vital parts of a ship's skeleton. Saw gangs could now come in and cut the ship's timbers whole in the needed shapes.

The boy knew these shapes as well as he knew anything. He had spent hours in the mold loft of the shipyards, where men lofted, or drew, on the floor the ship's important parts to their exact size and shape. He could visualize these shapes as quickly as he could the faces of his family. He knew the patterns far better than any school lesson he had ever been taught, for he was indeed a reader of the woods. He marked the tree with two slashes of his small hatchet for the saw gangs and moved on in the filtered light of the forest.

The forests that reached nearly to the ocean's edge provided the "bone" for American shipbuilding. There was white oak for the ship's keel, which ran like a spine along the middle of the ship's bottom from back to front, white pine for the decks, chestnut for posts and rails, spruce for the smaller spars such as the topgallant masts and yards, ash for blocks, locust for the treenails (the pegs used in fastening planks), hard pine for beams, and larch or hackmatack for knees and ribs.

Once the trees had been marked and cut, the timbers were hauled overland by horse or floated downriver to the shipyards. There was nothing simple about shipbuilding. Everything was done by hand, and the most important part of the process was people. Many different kinds of craftsmen were required, each as skillful in his job as the young woodsman was in scouting trees. There were carpenters, ropemakers, coopers (barrelmakers), sailmakers, caulkers (whose job it was to fill the seams between the planks to make a ship leakproof), and of course designers. They all worked with special hand tools, such as jack planes and adzes, that allowed them to shape timbers to perfect curves and measure within one-hundredth of an inch. There were no power saws or electric sanders in those days. If you could go back in time and visit a typical New England shipyard after a workday and hold up your lantern to the wall where the wooden-handled tools hung on pegs, you would notice that each handle had a particular luster —dark and rich—that seemed to have been coaxed out of the wood from its very heart. It is the sign of a tool well used over the years by knowing hands—the mark of a handcraftsman. Using only their own muscle power, skill, and intuition, these men shaped the timbers to build the ships that sailed the oceans of the world.

A ship is built from the bottom up, and just as a house needs a foundation, so does a ship. The keel is the foundation. Once the keel of a sailing ship was shaped and laid, the "floors" were attached to it. These were some of the angular pieces of wood for which the young woodsman had scanned the trees in the forest. Then to each end of the keel a curved section of wood was attached in a vertical position. The forward curved section was called the stem and the one at the back end of the ship the sternpost. These pieces were always strongest if the wood could be cut

16

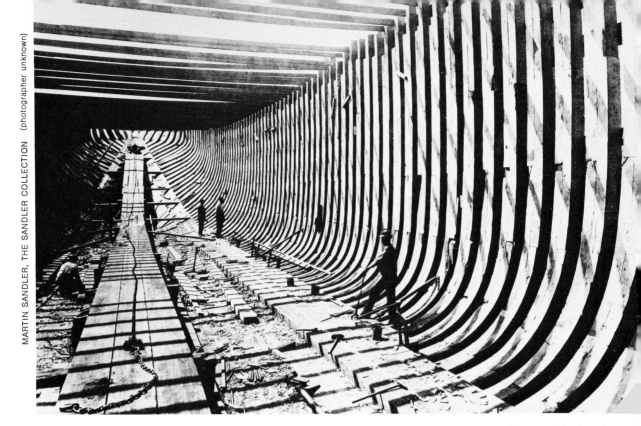

*The scarfed ribs of
a tall ship
under construction
in East Boston*

from one curving piece of a tree, perhaps a large branch that joined with the trunk of the tree in a smooth curve. But if the young woodsman could not find such a tree, the carpenters had to "scarf" pieces of wood together. Scarfing was a special way of joining straight pieces of wood to form a curve. It was done by cutting the ends of each piece of wood at an angle and then shaping them so that they would overlap and fit tightly together. Next the keelson was laid, directly above the first keel and resting on the floors. This was needed to give extra support and strength to the entire ship. Up to this point the structure looked more like a gigantic backbone than a ship, but after the keelson was in place the carpenters began work on the side curves of the ship's frame, which were made from scarfed pieces of wood called ribs. And just as ribs are to a human body, so are a ship's ribs to its hull, which is the ship's body. They provide the framing or shape for a ship. The ship was then given "skin," or a covering of boards. The interior of the covering boards was called ceiling; the exterior, planking. Between the seams of these boards the caulkers pounded in the oakum with their "beetles," or mauls, which were

17

heavy mallets, and a caulking iron, a wedge-shaped tool which pushed in the oakum. Oakum was made by soaking a ropy material in tar, which made it like a sticky tangle of hair perfect for keeping water from leaking through cracks. Hot pitch was then spread over the oakum caulking; once it had dried and hardened, it was scraped smooth.

When the hull of a ship was finished there was still much work to be done—masts and yards to be built, sails to be cut and sewn, ropes and lines to be made. The list seemed endless. It would often take a year to build a single ship, and this did not include the planning and design.

Sitting astride a log and paddling with hands and feet across a river, the first seaman hundreds of thousands of years ago faced the same problem that every sailor has faced since then: to move the log's cargo—in this case himself—from one side of the water to the other. After several attempts and successful trips, the first seaman probably struck upon the idea that he would be more comfortable if he sat *in* the log rather than *on* it. So he hollowed it out. Then perhaps he noticed how the chopped-off blunt ends of the log pushed the water, creating a wave that pressed back on the head of the log, thus slowing down his speed. The first seaman began to consider hewing the end of the log so that the whole log could slip through with less resistance and arrive at the other side faster. The simple log was developing into a more seaworthy container or vessel. Soon seamen began to think about ways of shaping the underwater part of the log to achieve even greater speed.

By the year 1832 there had been a lot of changes in ship design since that first seaman straddled his log. There were many theories about which shape was best for traveling through the water. A popular saying at the time was that a ship should have a cod's head and a mackerel's tail. A cod's head was full and a mackerel's tail thin and narrow. What was important was not how the ship entered the water but that its stern leave the water smooth behind. The spreading body of the ship was necessary for deepwater

18

Donald McKay, shipbuilder

sailing, it was thought, to prevent it from plunging too deeply into the ocean.

But not everybody felt this way. A few thought that these ships with their cod's heads and mackerel's tails sat on the water like tubs and moved like cows. In 1832 a young shipwright from Nova Scotia and his bride were living in a tiny cluttered apartment in New York City. Every single inch of wall space was covered with drawings of ships. The carpets had been rolled up and hull lines chalked in on the bare wood of the floors. In the evenings the young man, his wife, and their friend, another shipwright, would talk and plan and draw up their new designs. And these new designs in no way resembled cod's heads with mackerel's tails. Instead of being rounded or full in front, the prow, or forward section of the ship, curved in. It was designed to cut through the water like a knife. Donald McKay, his wife Albenia Boole, and their friend John Willis Griffiths had designed what were to be the most important changes in hull shapes in the thousand-year history of shipbuilding, changes that were to influence the entire future of ship design. But at that time nobody would listen to them or look at their designs. They were young, their ideas were strange

19

The Cutty Sark, *the only surviving clipper ship, in dry berth in Greenwich, England.*

and different, and few ship owners were willing to take a chance on new ideas. Eventually, however, when the competition for speed became fierce, these people got their chance through some shipbuilders and owners who had the vision to see the possibilities in their designs.

The peculiar concave prow lines and sharp-ended shapes that the three young people had laid down on paper and carved into hundreds of models in the McKays' living room were those of the fantastic clipper ships. These, instead of causing water to be "heaped up and pushed ahead of the vessel," as with a full cod's head–type ship, sliced through the water cleanly and with little resistance. As a result, the ship would sail much faster. It was John Griffiths who was given the chance to build the first true clipper, *Rainbow,* which astonished the world from her very launching because she did not tip over as so many had predicted. Later, she astonished critics again by her record passages to China.

20

But McKay's time was coming. The rivalry among owners for fast ships was increasing, for it was the first cargo into a port that drew the highest prices, and owners were willing to trade stowage space for speed. In partnership with William Currier of Newburyport, Massachusetts, McKay built the first ship of his own design —the *Currier*—three years before the *Rainbow* was launched. She was quite small and not a true clipper, but she hinted at the future with her longer and finer lines. She raced across the Atlantic on her runs to Rio de Janeiro in the coffee trade, outsailing every other ship. The maritime world could not help noticing the *Currier* and wondering about her young designer, who was then just thirty-two years old.

Enoch Train, a wealthy ship owner who wanted to build a line of packet ships for the Liverpool trade, sought out McKay. The first ship built for Train was the *Joshua Bates*, and it was McKay's design completely. Train never interfered after the contract had been signed. As the beautiful ship was launched and slid into the Merrimac River, Train knew he had been right in trusting the young designer. Right there on the riverbank Train turned to McKay and said, "You're coming to Boston. You're to build all my ships." McKay replied, "I'll come to Boston, and you'll have the best ships afloat."

Donald and Albenia moved their family to East Boston, and a year after Griffiths built *Rainbow*, McKay built the largest ship in the world to that date, named *New World*. But his first real clipper was not to be built until four years later, in 1849, when the country went crazy with gold fever, and people and goods could not be transported fast enough to California.

There were no railroads, and as California's population swelled, food, clothing, tools, and all kinds of supplies were desperately needed. Swift ships were the answer. There were profits to be made in a town like San Francisco in 1849 and 1850 when tea and coffee were four dollars a pound, eggs sold for a dollar apiece, and flour was forty dollars a barrel.

Staghound he christened her; she was McKay's first true clipper. She flashed around the Horn to San Francisco in a remark-

The launching of a McKay ship, Glory of the Seas, *at East Boston in 1869.*
The figure in the center, in top hat, back turned, is Donald McKay

able 108 days in spite of losing her main-topmast and topgallant mast in a storm. McKay followed *Staghound* with the *Flying Cloud*, often considered his most magnificent ship. Then came *Straffordshire*, *Sovereign of the Seas*, and the *Great Republic*, a masterpiece which burned shortly after launching. He continued to build, always refining his ideas and improving upon his designs.

The demand for huge clipper ships lessened toward the end of the Gold Rush, and McKay turned to designing smaller ships, each one a masterpiece. The shipbuilding boom eventually came to an end. There was no longer the need. Steam was the coming thing. Although in the wartime of 1865 McKay designed two steamers, there came a time when he could no longer afford to keep his East Boston yards open and had to find another way to support his family. He returned to Newburyport to farm.

McKay outlived all of his ships. They were all either burned or lost at sea. Even the precious models that he had carved himself had been burned for firewood by some thoughtless soul. In spite of this, McKay's and Griffith's notion of a concave prow that could cut the water rather than "heap it up" lives today in the lines of most seagoing cargo vessels.

When Donald McKay was an old man looking back on his career as a master designer, he remarked, "I have never yet built a vessel that came up to my own ideal. I saw something in each ship which I desired to improve upon."

Three

A designer knew a ship in one way, but a sailor had to have a special knowledge too, not just of the ship but of himself—of how well he'd be able to think and act in a dangerous situation, what he could make his body do when his mind was numb with fear. He had to know every part of himself and every part of the ship and how he and the ship fit together. His life depended on this knowledge and so did the safety of the ship and the lives of other sailors.

Life on board was not easy for any seaman, but for a young boy on his first voyage it could be terrible indeed. In a ship's articles, or list of crew members, he was identified simply as "boy" and was expected to do everything from scrubbing the decks to furling the skysails. Being the youngest and the most inexperienced, he often endured cruel taunting from the other crew members in the fo'c'sle (the forecastle, or seamen's quarters). It was always easiest to blame the boy for something, because being the smallest he could not fight back. For a boy, life on a tall ship could sometimes seem like the meanest trick ever invented.

Captain E. P. Nichols once wrote:

When a boy gets it into his mind that he wants to go to sea, he only looks at the sunny side—(even that is not very bright)—and sees the sailor on his return from a long voyage flush with money, apparently having a joyful time, but he does not think of the deprivation that man had had while away at sea; . . . our advice to any boy is: let the sea alone: seek any other occupation . . . our advice to any parent that has a boy bent on going to sea is: reason

Captain Edward Payson Nichols (1844–90), who wrote and published the humorous newspaper Ocean Chronicles *while at sea*

with him and try to show him just how foolish he is . . . but if after all your prayers and entreaties he still holds to the idea of going, take him gently by the arm and lead him out behind the barn and —knock him on the head.

That strategy just did not work with Charles Augustus Abbey. It is not known for sure if his father ever knocked him on the head, but he tried his best to persuade young Charles to stay home and continue his studies so that someday he might become a teacher. In 1856, when he was only fourteen years old, Charles shipped on the clipper *Surprise* for the Penang Islands off the Malay Peninsula, then for Singapore, Hong Kong, and Canton. For seventeen out of his first twenty days at sea Charles, or "Abbey," as the crew called him, was miserably seasick. Almost every day in the first three weeks his diary begins with the words "I really feel quite sick today" or "Feel very weak today" or "Not well at all." By the end of the second week he wrote: "I have this day made up my mind that if I ever get to the good port of New York again and find my father alive I will fall to anything he may set me to and pursue it with as much diligence as possible."

Abbey had to do every kind of task including what he de-

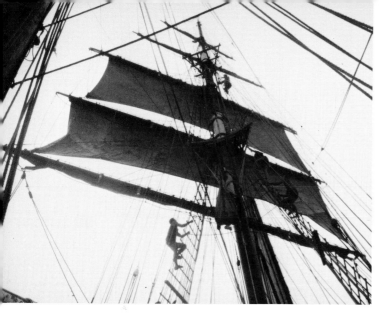

To make one's way to the top royal was a daring journey. A sailor first had to swing up into the ratlines between the rigging and then climb, hand over hand, to the point where the lower mast meets the topmast, then haul himself over the crosstrees

He continued from the topmast upward to the top gallant, reached out for the next set of crosstrees, told himself not to look down, and kept a sharp eye on the royal yard

Once at the royal yard, he swung out onto the footropes strung just below the yard

Between the crew and death were some ropes, their own muscles, and steady nerves. In sunlight or pitch-black night, in hurricane or blizzard, they went aloft, climbing swiftly through the gigantic web

scribed as the "dirtyest, nastyest and stickiest work" of slushing down the rigging. This involved coating all the lines of the yards with a mixture of tar and oil that protected them from rotting. His head might feel dizzy from having vomited his last two meals, but because he was the lightest in weight, Abbey was a favorite for the job of furling the royals and skysails. He described in his diary some of his trips to the top:

May 3, 1856

I feel very weak today but I "turned to" this evening. I furled a skysail for the first time and I thought I should fail before I got to the yard I was so weak.

He described having to take a line aloft to the royal yard to thread it through a block. It is difficult enough simply to climb up a mast to a point eighty-feet above the deck without carrying something.

May 17, 1856

The way I managed it was thus. I made a bowline (a kind of knot) on one end and put it over my shoulder (so that I could use both hands) and then shinnied about 30 feet on two ropes and rove it through a block at the end of the royal mast head and then I had to take the bare end and creep out on the yard (a ticklish place) and laid flat holding on with my feet and rove it through another block as far out as it possibly could have been hung. When done I had barely strength to hold onto the rigging. . . . A dull heavy sea sent the yard first to one side then the other with a jerk hard enough to send you off the yard if you didn't dig your fingernails into the wood and my shoes having just been greased I could not manage to do anything for a long time. But at last a sailor shouted up from the deck 85 feet below, "Sling one arm over the royal brace, Abbey."

The seamen on the *Surprise* were decent enough fellows and tried to help Abbey out when he was in trouble, but unfortunately the

second mate was a brutal man who would often beat the boys for no real reason.

Abbey spent a lot of time on that first voyage making promises to an absent father and dreaming about roast beef dinners when all there was to eat was salt pork and moldy biscuits. But he did make it to China and back home while recalling in his diary the words of Richard Henry Dana, who had shipped out as a boy and written about his experiences in a book that Abbey had read, *Two Years Before the Mast*. The words and idea were simple enough: "I knew it could not last always so I stuck it out and finished it." But for many it was never "finished." For some reason boys were drawn back to the sea and to voyages time and time again, despite the hardships. Boys who went to sea at ten or eleven grew into old men without having spent more than twenty days of their lives on land after signing for their first voyage. The deepwater sailing ships became their homes, and in between, when they were "on the beach," they would stay in sailors' boardinghouses. Their only possessions were carried in a sea bag which might contain a change of underwear, a pair of trousers, a shirt, a Bible, a knife, a fid—a wood spike for rope work—and a sail needle.

To be a seaman required knowledge and skill. An ordinary seaman had to be able to keep his balance and his nerves aloft. He had to be good with his hands in everything from sewing to splicing ropes and rigging. He had to be skillful at the wheel, for if he

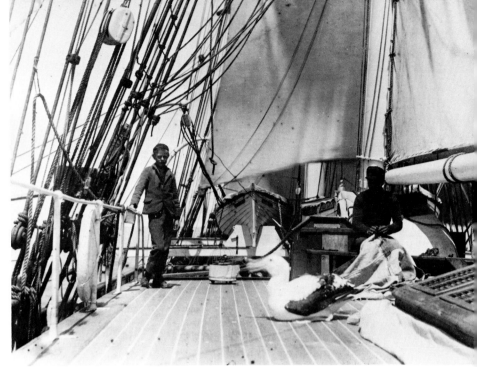

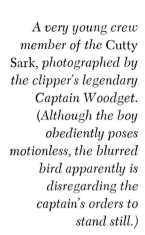

A very young crew member of the Cutty Sark, *photographed by the clipper's legendary Captain Woodget. (Although the boy obediently poses motionless, the blurred bird apparently is disregarding the captain's orders to stand still.)*

brought a ship too close to the wind a sail could shake and knock a man out of the rigging. Sloppy work on a tall ship could result in death. He also had to make do with little. He had to wash his clothes in a half-bucket of water and eat what remained of the hardtack after he had knocked the weevils out of it. To pass the time, he might whittle a ship model from a discarded beef bone. Finally, he had to be able to live with others in uncomfortably cramped quarters. An ordinary seaman might have a space totaling seven feet in length and two feet in width which he could call his own. Neatness, cleanliness, and manners were the mark of an experienced seaman because they were necessary for survival in the fo'c'sle.

If he knew how to read, write, and do figures, worked hard at learning navigation, and had a sense of leadership, a young seaman could work his way up through the ranks becoming an officer and perhaps someday a captain. But there were many excellent sailors who were content to remain ordinary seamen all of their lives. They preferred the feel of the rigging between their palms to that of a sextant; they preferred the chanteys of deck work and the jokes of the fo'c'sle to the giving of orders and the making of gentlemanly conversation at the captain's table.

Left: *The crew of the* Gork Foch *hauling the braces*

Below: *A sailor has slung his hammock on deck to escape the heat of the fo'c'sle*

Left: *A chore for spare moments is "whipping" or binding the ends of ropes to prevent fraying*

Below: *Helmsman keeps a sharp lookout for wind changes as he steers the* Regina Maris

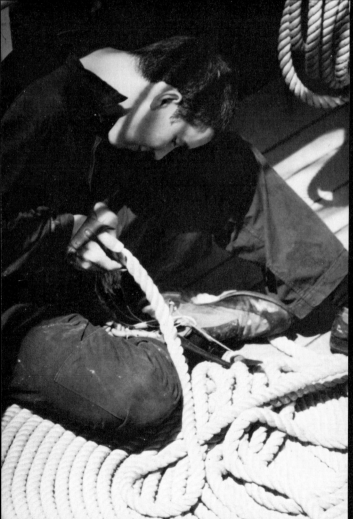

The Gork Foch *sails close-hauled off Bermuda*

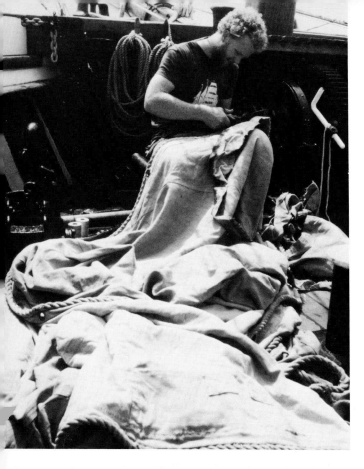

A *sailor aboard the* Regina Maris
mends canvas

The sailmaker was often the oldest man on board a tall ship. With no pattern other than a list of figures and no fancy tools other than a needle and thread, he turned thousands of feet of canvas into precisely made sails. He was the master deep-sea tailor, the provider of the one most crucial part in the power system of these tall wind ships.

His work room was usually the flat roof of the midship deckhouse, but even there he didn't have enough space to spread the entire sail at one time. He seemed to work mainly by instinct, although he did have his book of figures to determine the number of degrees off a right angle the sides of the sail needed to be to give it a nice belly for the wind to fill. Seated on a low bench beside the deckhouse roof, he sewed, moving along the bench as his stitches progressed. Grommets were punched into one side for lashing the sail to the yard, and leather was used to reinforce the lower corners for attaching the sheet tackle. The sailmaker worked long hours, especially when the weather was good. If the ship was a Cape Horner, he often made a complete new set of extra heavy sails before reaching the Horn.

Equally important in maintaining the ship was the carpenter. Although wood was the material he handled most often, he was skillful and ready to work with everything from iron to shark bone. It was the carpenter's responsibility to repair, patch, and rebuild all the thousands of things that broke down during a voyage. If a rudder snapped in a gale while the ship was rounding Cape Horn, the carpenter would stand at his vise bench, often tied in to prevent his being washed overboard, and begin to build a substitute before the ship crashed on the point of Tierra del Fuego or fetched up on a reef off Staten Island. He had to be prepared to work in the most violent weather to repair holes in the hull of a ship and broken spars, to make new treenails or refashion oar blades. Herman Melville in his novel *Moby Dick* lists among the carpenter's tasks and skills those of making birdcages for lost land birds that fly aboard, mixing up soothing lotions for a sailor's strained muscles, painting decorations on oars and other ship equipment, piercing sailors' ears so they could wear shark bone earrings, and pulling teeth. The carpenter was absolutely cunning with a pocketknife, chisel, and piece of wood, and, as Melville wrote, "His brain . . . must have oozed along into the muscles of his fingers."

The cook had no refrigerator, no canned goods. Fresh food and livestock could only be carried for short periods. There were no such things as airtight plastic containers, and no way to keep breads from getting moldy and infested with weevils and other bugs. All meats were salted heavily, for this was the only known method of preservation. In those days to be a cook on a ship was the hardest and most thankless job of all, for the cook had little to work with in his galley—and much to work against: dampness, bugs, heat, mold, filth.

The cooks in those days were often runaway slaves and were sometimes terribly abused, but it was not for their lack of skill. It was nearly impossible to serve up good meals at sea in the 1800s when all the basics one had to work with were hardtack (a biscuit as hard as a stone), salted beef or pork called "salt junk," flour, molasses, water, and "slush," or grease. The cook often combined these things into mysterious mixtures. "Scouse," for example, was soaked hardtack, salt pork, and molasses baked in a pan. "Duff" was flour, water, and dried fruit mixed together and "boiled down hard and heavy as lead" in a canvas bag. Before hardtack biscuit could be eaten, one had to knock out the weevils by rapping it sharply on the table. The creatures would come crawling out in streams from their dry nutritious havens, and a sailor had to wait until the premises were vacated before he could begin to gnaw on his biscuit.

A key figure in the operation of the ship was the mate. His job was to supervise the crew in all deck work so that all the captain's commands could be carried out. Many ships had a first and a second mate. The crew was divided into watches or groups, each under the direction of a mate. Mates chose the sailors for their groups on the first day. (The word *watch* was also used to indicate the time periods during which the men worked on deck.)

Every noon and evening when the weather was clear, the captain and the first mate appeared on deck to perform one of the day's most mysterious rituals. Each man peered at the sun or a star through an odd-looking instrument while muttering numbers and strange words. After a few moments of writing figures on a piece of paper, they disappeared below to work out the combinations that would, as if by magic, determine the position of the ship at sea, telling them how far they were from Calcutta or Canton or wherever they wanted to go. To the ordinary seaman navigation seemed more magical than scientific. It was, however, a mate's responsibility to teach navigation to young apprentice seamen who were willing to learn. If the mate was a good man and a skillful teacher, a boy could learn a lot, but many mates were impressed with their own power and more interested in giving orders than in teaching.

In the late eighteenth century there was one mate, perhaps the most famous in sailing history, who wanted to give something more

The carpenter and first mate of the nineteenth-century Great Admiral

to the men on his watch. As a result of his efforts to teach ordinary seamen simplified methods of navigation, this complicated science was made more understandable to the whole world. He also made the numbers and celestial tables on which lives depended more exact than ever before. Mate Nathaniel Bowditch's contribution to the safety of a sailing ship was every bit as remarkable and important as the invention of radar more than one hundred fifty years later.

There were two ways to navigate a ship: by "log, lead, and lookout" and by celestial navigation. A navigator using the first

The captain and officers of the schooner D. H. Rivers *"shoot the sun"
to determine their noon position*

method simply kept track of distance traveled by towing a "log line" which rotated as the ship moved through the water. "Lead" refers to the lead line which was dropped into the water to indicate the depth and any underwater danger that could not be seen. The lookout was a sailor posted in the crow's nest to keep an eye out for land.

The second method of navigating was more complicated and in some ways more exact. By measuring the angle between the horizon and the noon sun with a sextant, a navigator could calculate latitude—the distance north or south of the equator. But when Nathaniel Bowditch took his first voyage, there was no easy way to find longitude—the distance east or west of an imaginary line that ran north and south through Greenwich, a borough in London, England. How far a ship was to the east or west of the Greenwich meridian was figured by time with a clock called a chronometer. The clock was set at Greenwich Time, and because every twenty-four hours the earth turns around once, the sun seems to be rising somewhere all the time. When it is sunset in Greenwich, at another place halfway around the world it will be sunrise, and one-fourth of the way around the world it will be midnight. By using a chronometer set at Greenwich Time and by checking the time of noon or sunrise at the ship's position, it could be figured how far the ship was from an imaginary line through Greenwich, because it was known exactly how many miles the earth turns each hour. However accurate, chronometers were terribly expensive and few ships in Bowditch's day could afford them.

There was a second way of finding the distance east or west of the Greenwich meridian. It was called a lunar and could be figured without a chronometer. The problem with this method was that it required complicated mathematical calculations that took days to figure out. By that time a ship was no longer in the same position. With lunars it was also necessary to catch the moon "occulting," or crossing in front of, a very bright star, a rare occurrence.

On one of his early voyages Bowditch figured out a simple way to do lunars. Instead of waiting for the moon to occult a star, he determined the moon's position in relation to three stars, a method that could be used at any time the stars were visible. This was his first big contribution to navigation. An even more important step was his logarithmic tables which simplified the complicated trigonometric calculations. Using the tables, anyone who could add and subtract could work out any navigation problem because Bowditch had already done all the difficult figuring and nothing more was needed except addition and subtraction. Any seaman in the fo'c'sle could now learn navigation.

Bowditch began his lessons with the men in the fo'c'sle on his first voyage in 1795. He believed that all the crew had a right to learn and that navigation should not be reserved for officers. The men Bowditch taught during the long watches not only felt a deep respect for him but also gained a new respect for themselves. As a mate Nathaniel Bowditch was not just a leader of men but a maker of leaders. Any sailor who could say, "I sailed with Bowditch," had the password to an officer's berth on any ship.

Among the responsibilities of the mate was the supervision of "tacking." To tack, or change the direction of a ship, was a complex job requiring several steps all carried out with utmost precision. The command to tack was first given by the captain to the first mate. The first mate then waited for just the right moment to begin the maneuver. He had to find an easing of the wind, often just by the feel of it on his face, before calling out the next order, which would send into action eight or more men and boys. The captain stood on the deck above the mate, and behind the mate might be a boy studying the mate's posture, the set of his shoulders, the way he clasped and unclasped his hands behind his back, the subtle shift of weight from one foot to the other. An experienced sailor observing the mate could almost anticipate the second the next order would be given. The mate might tilt his chin up and catch sight of the shadow of a ruffle in the royals. If the crew was observant, they knew a decision had been made and they were ready to spring into action before the order came: "Ready about!"

The boy standing behind the mate already had his hands on the royal braces. Another boy ran to take care of the slack in the topgallant braces. For the heavier work four men were put on each brace. The sailmaker and the carpenter went forward to handle the jib sheets; the cook stood ready at the foresheet near his galley.

The mate's first order had stationed the men. Now the second order was given: "Lee-ho, down helm!"

The wheel was spun toward the direction of the wind. The rudder steered the ship windward. The sailmaker and the carpenter loosened the jib sheets, while the cook loosened the foresheet. The spanker was hauled up to push the bow of the ship even more into the wind. There was a great noise of flapping canvas as the wind spilled from all the sails. The ship's speed slowed as she swung across the wind. Then just as the ship's bowsprit was crossing the direction from which the wind was coming, the mate shouted, "Mainsail haul!" This meant that all hands were to work the lines of the yards of the mainmast and the mizzenmast by hauling in the braces. They did this as fast as they could while the young boys, lighter in weight and not as strong, took in the slack of the smaller braces hand over hand. The yards were then trimmed or adjusted more finely. The fore and aft staysails were "sheeted"

The helmsman begins the tacking maneuver by spinning the wheel to turn the ship into the wind

Sailors haul on braces . . .

. . . bringing the sail around

Tacking accomplished, the deck is neatened and the line carefully coiled on a belaying pin

by pulling their ropes, called sheets, to the other side, which was the new downwind side of the vessel, or the lee side. The wind now coming from the new windward side of the ship filled the main and mizzen.

The sails on the foremast which had not been eased from the tack before the ship came around were aback with the wind on the wrong side of them and were holding the ship like a giant brake, but they pushed the bow around toward the new direction. "Let go and haul!" shouted the mate, and the foremast sails were finally released. The men furiously hauled in on the braces to take in the slack, and things were set for the ship to leap forward once more with all sails full on the wind's way.

40

A sailor relaxes in a hammock

The captain retired to his cabin. The deck looked like a great tangle of spaghetti, but in no time, under the mate's supervision, every line was coiled and in its place.

In those days life on a tall ship was thought to be for men only. Sometimes a captain brought along his wife and daughters, but men considered it unlucky to sail with women. Still, for every bad-luck story about women on board ship, there was a good story.

An expert navigator and one of the bravest seawomen ever was Mary Patten, wife of the captain of a tall ship. Her husband caught a terrible fever and became blind in the middle of a storm off Cape Horn. The first mate was being held in irons for insubordination, and no other man on board knew how to navigate. Mary Patten, still a teenager, had learned this science on previous voyages. Though she was small and not very strong, for fifty-two days she navigated a clipper ship nearly two hundred feet long and weighing more than sixteen hundred tons. She took the clipper safely into San Francisco harbor, its destination.

Emily Woolridge, wife of the captain of the *Maid of Athens*, accompanied her husband on a voyage to California. They were shipwrecked on Staten Island on their way to rounding Cape Horn. For more than a month Emily Woolridge lived and worked on this uninhabited island. She worked alongside the men, wearing a gunny sack for warmth, and together they built a boat to sail to the Falkland Islands. She ate penguin, nursed her desperately sick husband, kept discipline among the crew, and always showed courage even in despair. In her diary she wrote of her experience on the island:

> Early during the morning I went down to the cascade to bathe my eyes and face, but having only a pocket handkerchief to bathe and dry with was not comfortable. I thought of them all at home in carpeted bedrooms, and I at a running stream, stooping on a stone without a roof or anything but trees to cover me at night. I, who was thought so delicate at home, but still we had much to be thankful for.

Although the wife of Captain Nichols found life at sea often frightening and difficult, her two daughters, Nannie and Maude, who accompanied their parents on the long voyages, seemed to have had a good time and, like so many children who went to sea, found a ship forever fascinating. The captain and his wife wrote a little about how Nannie and Maude spent their days. For example, Captain Nichols described one event:

> Nannie and Maude took a bath at three o'clock in the morning. Their window was open and the vessel gave a heavy roll which put the window all the way under, and the water came in . . . and deposited about twenty gallons on their berth, striking them on

the face and stomach. They both began to sing but on different key; one on C sharp; the other on B flat.

In addition to taking a bath in the wee hours, the children helped the sailmaker make a new sail, gave singing concerts, and practiced the piano which was kept in the saloon. Once in a while they did their lessons, but Captain Nichols felt that he was the world's worst teacher:

> I was never built for a teacher. . . . I call the spelling class; they spell "Kat" with a "c," "dorg" without "r" and put an "r" and "e" in "hoss." I send them back to their seat and mark "spelling imperfect." I call the grammar class and say, "Is you all here?" And they answer "we am."

For the most part a child's schooling at sea meant listening to sailors' yarns for literature class, practicing complicated knots and etching designs on bone for arts and crafts, learning celestial navigation for arithmetic lessons, and climbing the rigging for gym.

In spite of all the work on a tall ship, there were many long hours when the men had nothing to do. Sailors were ingenious at devising activities for their spare time. They seemed to have a gift for working with their hands, and many of them crafted intricate model ships using everything from chicken bones to wood. Also popular were two-foot-long pipes carved from the wing bones of albatrosses or elegantly sculpted canes and walking sticks from shark's backbones. These backbones were often collected by the dangerous pastime of shark wrestling. The men fished for sharks using a piece of old salt beef for bait. When the shark swallowed the bait, they hauled it on board. The contest was now ready to begin. The object was to see how long a man could ride the thrashing body of the shark and keep all his fingers. It was said that if a shark was able to curl his tail underneath the man, the ride was over, for the shark could flip the man right off. But it was worse to be slapped by the tail, which could lash out and break a man's back. A quieter activity was scrimshaw—engraving ivory, whale bone, or sperm whale teeth—perhaps the best known of the sailor's arts. Designs ranged from portraits of lady friends left behind to full-rigged ships sailing through a stormy sea.

Captains, too, found time passing slowly and often took up hobbies and crafts to while away the hours. Captain Richard Woodget, master of the unbeatable *Cutty Sark*, one of the fastest clippers, never let the fact that a ship is a constantly rolling platform interfere with the pursuit of his favorite pastimes, among which was roller-skating in the 'tween decks when this space was empty of cargo. He took great joy in teaching his officers this exhilarating sport, and many a day as *Cutty Sark* tore across the oceans of the world in all her splendor there rose from the open hatches the rumble of Woodget and his officers madly roller-skating. On one run, as a switch from roller-skating, Woodget took up bicycling. Another of his hobbies was photography. Many mates dreaded the order to accompany Woodget on one of his photographic expeditions, for this meant being put overboard in a lifeboat with Woodget and his ancient camera in midocean. For this operation two lifeboats were usually lashed together and a plank placed across them to support the camera on its tripod. After much fussing about with equipment and numerous orders as to exactly how the lifeboats should be angled and held in the sea, Woodget would manage to get a shot of the *Cutty Sark* under sail thousands of miles from land.

For a man who had been away months and sometimes years, the very thought of land was an exciting thing. A sailor could hardly wait to get ashore, even if he didn't speak the language of the port of call or have a home or family there. Yet these ordinary seamen were not comfortable on land. They often seemed like an odd sort to land folks. They spoke a language of their own, full of special words and phrases. On deck, where they spent most of their time, words meant action—precise action on which lives depended. "Sling one leg over the royal brace, Abbey!" or "Haul in the main brace" or "Cat the anchor," "All hands shorten sail," "Brail up the

The clipper
Cutty Sark *under*
full sail in a
photograph taken by
her master,
Captain Woodget

royals," "Clew up," "Haul down," "Reef the fore-topsail," "Down helm," "Hove to"—all were strange-sounding phrases and words that had no meaning on land. It was hard for a sailor returning to port to enter into the easy chatter and social conversation of land folks.

As soon as the anchor was down, many of the men were off spending their money and drinking themselves into a stupor. In such a condition they were hardly welcomed by the land folks, except for saloon keepers and crimps. Crimps shanghaied, or kidnapped, sailors. They specialized in getting sailors drunk with liquor and promises of money. When the sailor was so drunk he knew nothing or passed out, the crimp would haul him off to another ship in need of a crew. He could receive as much as a hundred and fifty dollars for each man he delivered. A sailor filled with high hopes for a good time on land would find himself within twelve hours shipping out again for another long voyage. Time and again sailors were caught by the crimps. It seems odd that they never learned. Perhaps, despite all their excitement at the prospect of land life, they also experienced a feeling of uneasiness or insecurity when their feet touched earth. They may have sensed deep inside that for them a sailing ship was their only real home.

45

Four

Searsport, Maine, in 1840 was a one-street town, and that street was made not of cobblestones, but of dirt. There were almost three hundred inhabitants. Among the modest frame houses were perhaps three or four larger, more impressive buildings set far back from the street. There were two wharves, a sail loft, a blacksmith's shop, and at one time eleven shipyards. There were also two churches, a school, a lumber mill, a grist mill, and three taverns, and outside the town probably some of the worst farming country in the United States. There was absolutely nothing remarkable about Searsport except one thing: At a certain time in its history one-tenth of all the tall-ship captains in the United States came from there. By some mystery or quirk of fate this plain little town produced masters of the deep water—many of them youths who became tall-ship captains before their twentieth birthdays.

Captain Andrew Sherburne Pendleton must have known his destiny from boyhood. When a full-rigged ship was tied up in Searsport on a moonless night, young Andrew would slip aboard and climb quickly through the spidery web of ropes and spars. At the royal yard he'd stop to rest, letting the darkness wrap itself around him, dangling his feet into the black night. It was a nice feeling in this simplified place of ropes and wood, as if all the forces of the world for a few moments were in a state of rare and beautiful balance. Inevitably a voice would boom from below, "Damn you lad. I see you! Git yerself down here before ye smash the deck with your thick skull, or I'll flog you within an inch of yer life!" And as the boy scrambled for the ratlines and made his way down,

A journey to the top begins in the webbing of the ratlines

47

The main street of Searsport

a voice in his own head would be pounding even louder: "Could I do it in a gale off Cape Horn? Could I do it in a gale off the Horn? Could I climb that high?"

At the age of eleven, on one of his slides through a web of rope and wood, Andrew Pendleton made a decision. He would not go back to school. He would go to sea. His father had been lost at sea the year before, but this did not make Andrew unusual. Plenty of boys had lost fathers at sea. It did not stop them from seeking out a

A full gale blows and four men work aloft taking in sail aboard the bark
Garthsnaid. *The second most dangerous place to be was where the
photographer stood, on deck where one could easily be swept overboard*

berth aboard a vessel which would take them away from home for years. So that year Andrew Pendleton left school and his home to go to sea as a cook on a coastal schooner.

Between the ages of eleven and eighteen, he advanced from cook to captain. His first command was a coastal schooner, the *Frederick and William*. But it was not long until he was commanding tall ships across the Atlantic and around the Horn to California and the Far East for the Canton trade.

He married Nancy Pendleton Carver, a relative, and she accompanied him on many voyages. Their daughter Marietta was born aboard the bark *Thomas Fletcher* off the coast of Wales, and Captain Pendleton himself delivered the baby. When someone asked him later if he had been nervous about the delivery, he said not really, but he had worried about having a silk thread which was necessary for tying off the umbilical cord—and for months after Marietta's birth he kept finding bits and pieces of silk thread in his pockets.

During a homeward-bound voyage from Shanghai, a young gentleman named Fred Essex shipped aboard the *Emma T. Crowell* as a paying passenger. In the journal he kept, he provided the only known firsthand account of Captain Pendleton in command of a ship. From his journal we can begin to understand better the character of a good captain. Of Pendleton he wrote:

> In person well favored and bearded, with the bright watchful eyes of a good mariner and the kind open smile and hearty manner of the sailor with all the traits of a natural born gentleman. A sort of simple and outdated man who before he reads his chapter of the bible every night sits down and asks himself whether he has wronged any man; who makes it his boast that not the meanest sailor aboard his ship but of whose comfort he makes a study, within the bounds of a discipline of the most perfect kind which he seems to maintain by simple kindness.

A captain had to know his men if the ship was to be a happy one. There is another true story of a captain who found himself in the

Captain Andrew Pendleton (wearing hat), indulging in one of his favorite shoretime activities, having his picture taken with friends

port of Geelong, Australia, at the height of a gold rush. His crew was wild with dreams of finding gold, and the captain knew they would desert ship for the gold fields. If that happened there would not be enough hands to take the ship home again to England with its return cargo, for hiring crew in this part of the world was difficult and expensive. What was the captain to do? Lock up all the crew? Or lay off shore never letting a man touch foot on land? Finally the captain decided that the most reasonable course of action was to call a meeting of the men and make a bargain. He told his men that he knew they were planning to desert ship and head for the gold fields. He described to them the difficulties of survival —life in the gold fields would be as tough as life at sea, the cost of food and shelter and tools would be very high, and so on. But if

51

they would all go together as a team, with himself as captain on land as he was at sea, and bring supplies from the ship, they might have a chance of finding some gold and surviving as well. They would prospect for two months and then return to the ship. Since they were taking ship supplies paid for by the owners, it would not be fair to take wages too, and if they did find gold it was only right that part of their share be given to the owners.

The men thought the plan fair and agreed to it immediately. They went off to the gold fields, and indeed they did find gold—quite a bit. A few crew members did desert when it came time to return to the ship. The captain again made a wise decision that avoided trouble among the loyal crewmen. He would divide the deserters' pay among them for the trip home. The ship arrived home on schedule with a happy crew, its intended cargo, plus a bonus of seven pounds of gold dust for the owners.

A captain had to understand his ship as well as his men and have the judgment to know what it could or could not do. During one voyage home from Shanghai, Captain Pendleton's bark, the *Emma T. Crowell*, was struck by a typhoon with winds well over a hundred miles an hour. She was dismasted, and nothing was more deadly on a ship than broken spars thrashing about wildly in a storm. They could kill people and rip up a deck and hull within seconds. The captain ordered all hands on deck with hatchets and axes into the dangerous stampede of rigging and masts that had been uprooted by the typhoon-force winds. Parts of the spars were rolling across the decks or dragging alongside the ship, threatening the hull. Captain and crew, working side by side, cut the spars away, but not before Pendleton's son was caught by a mast which rolled over his legs, breaking them both.

In the morning, after the typhoon had passed, the *Emma T. Crowell*, broken and crippled, drifted aimlessly in the China Sea like the stunned survivor of a bloody battle. The steam tugs from Shanghai chugged out to tow her back into port. But they were refused! The price was too high, and Captain Pendleton, knowing that his ship was no longer in any immediate danger, figured that he could direct his carpenter to make an emergency substitute

52

A painting of the Emma T. Crowell *dismasted in the China Sea*
(Collection of William Pendleton)

called a jury-rig and sail the *Crowell* into Shanghai himself. He proceeded to do just that. Eventually the tugs did help him for the last few miles after a lower price was negotiated.

Andrew Pendleton wrote long letters home to his friends and relatives describing details of ship life. These letters show his understanding of a ship and the ingenuity that made him a superior captain. He not only gave orders but did much of the actual work himself. In one letter headed "January 16, 1898, latitude 28:20 North; longitude 27:30 West," which located him at the time of the writing somewhere near the Canary Islands in the Atlantic, he described his problems with a leak:

> The first two weeks out the ship commenced to leak. We could not keep sail on her as I would like to . . . had to run her off so much to pump her out. . . . I see that we did not make so much water when on the starboard tack so thought the leak was on the starboard side above the water. It was so much sea in the doldrums that we could not do anything over the side but on 8° south put ship on starboard tack with main topsail to mast and as I had been looking everytime I could along the side I saw a butt [hole] about one inch under the copper. So got a stage over, with sticks lashed on, a caulking iron and top maul, tried the butt and in went the iron. Could not caulk it. It was too rough. So drove in a white pine wedge and the ship does not make more than 100 [pumping strokes] per 24 hours when she was making 160 per hour before. I was blue enough [from working in the cold water] I assure you.

When indeed there was time to be lazy, when all the letters home had been written, when there were no immediate decisions to be made and he was bored playing whist with his fellow officers, Captain Pendleton often turned to his favorite pastimes, knitting and lacemaking. He made hundreds of pairs of knitted slippers for relatives and a tablecloth that is a masterpiece of fine lacework.

There were times of great loneliness at sea for Andrew Pendleton. His letters home would sometimes be streaked with despair and frustration. He voiced deep concern over a brutal second mate, guilt over orders during the Spanish American War for merchant

54

A lace tablecloth made by Captain Pendleton on one of his voyages

ships to fly British flags for protection in certain waters, and worries about his family left behind in Searsport. He never became a really famous captain nor a rich one, for he was born too late to command the California gold clippers that brought huge salaries for their captains. Pendleton's total income for a year might have been barely one thousand dollars. Yet he chose this as his life's work—slashing through typhoons in the China Sea, storming around the Horn, coaxing a vessel through the windless doldrums —voyage after voyage to Shanghai, Calcutta, Geelong, River Platte, San Francisco, always on sailing ships.

Five

In the year 1871 more than one thousand tall ships entered the port of Boston alone. Then, at the end of the nineteenth century, shipyards started building steamships, and over the years many of the old tall ships disappeared. When steam came, the tall ships melted away like snow ships. For many ships the end was sad. Often their towering masts and yards were cut down. Their hulls, designed to slip through the water as naturally as dolphins, were no longer cared for and became scarred and shabby. Worst of all, some of the old tall ships were used as barges and finished out their lives on the ends of tow ropes being tugged along coastal routes, never again to run free with a fresh wind under a cloud of white sail. Some, however, were saved by sea-loving countries where the people knew that only in a tall sailing ship could young sailors learn the ways of the wind and sea.

In the summer of 1976 most of the tall ships that were left in the world were brought together for the greatest sailing race ever. There was the bark *Sagres* from Portugal, the ship *Dar Pomorza* from Poland, the barkentine *Regina Maris* from Boston, the *Nippon Maru* from Japan, the *Kruzenstern* from Russia, the *Christian Radich* from Norway, and many more. They started in Plymouth, England, and sailed to the Canary Islands, then across the Atlantic to Bermuda, and from Bermuda to Newport, Rhode Island.

They sailed to many of the great ports on the eastern seaboard, and when they paraded up the Hudson in New York, there were traffic jams as people rushed to the riverbanks to see the ships.

And then at last the tall ships came back to Boston, just as they had years ago in the days of the China trade. In the earliest hours of the morning before the sun was up and while the wind was still blowing out of the west, the old port city started to stir. Some people climbed onto rooftops high above Boston Harbor for a better view; others carried chairs into the waterfront streets. Out of roof skylights, opened for the first time in years, poked hundreds of heads. And in the harbor, strings of pennants flew like butterflies from the masts and rigging of five thousand small boats.

JOHN E. THAYER

58

A tough old battleship, the *Constitution*, glided out of the harbor like a proud queen—but one too old to move by herself. A red-and-black tugboat on each side gently swept her forward on her mission. Her masts raked back, her rigging like black lace against a blue sky, "Old Ironsides," as she is called, went out to greet the tall ships nearing the harbor entrance.

The yardarms and bowsprits of every ship were lively with men and women aloft waving at half a million people on shore singing and cheering. But there were those who could not speak, who stood quietly with wonder and a breath caught in their throats at the sight of the tall ships coming back to Boston—one by one by one.

Index